WAR AND EMANCIPATION.

A THANKSGIVING SERMON,

PREACHED IN THE

PLYMOUTH CHURCH, BROOKLYN, N. Y.

On Thursday, November 21, 1861.

BY

REV. HENRY WARD BEECHER.

TEXT.—"And after a time he returned to take her, and he turned aside to see the carcase of the lion: and behold, there was a swarm of bees and honey in the carcase of the lion."—JUDGES xiv. 8.

PHILADELPHIA:
T. B. PETERSON & BROTHERS,
No. 306 CHESTNUT STREET.

THE HONEY IN THE LION'S CARCASE.

A THANKSGIVING SERMON,

ON THE

WAR AND EMANCIPATION,

PREACHED BY

REV. HENRY WARD BEECHER,

AT THE

PLYMOUTH CHURCH, BROOKLYN,

November 21st, 1861.

Sampson was on an errand of love. He was interrupted by a lion, which he slew, for love is stronger than any lion. He gained his suit. Alas! everything went by contraries. Thereafter, the woman whose love was sweeter to him than honey at first, betrayed him; she was his lion; whereas, on his way home he found that bees had possession of the real lion's carcase, and had filled it with honey, and so in the end the lion was better to him than his wife.

But how full of suggestions is this incident! Who

would have looked for honey in a lion's caul? While he was yet roaring and striking at Sampson, there seemed very little likelihood of his finding a honeyed meal out of him; but if lions bravely slain yield such food, then let them become emblems!

The bee signifies industry among all nations, and honey is the very ideal of sweetness. To-day war is upon us, a lion is on our path, but being bravely met, in its track shall industry settle, and we shall yet fetch honey from the carcase of war. You will not object then, if to-day I bring you honey from this lion's body. At first, and to unhopeful souls, it would seem as if no day of thanksgiving ever was so sadly planted. Nor will I undertake to persuade you that there are no evils to bemoan. There are many; but the evils are transient, superficial and vincible,—the benefits are permanent, radical, and multiplying. Not long ago we were a united nation. Our industry was bringing in riches as the tides of the ocean, and no man could imagine the manhood of a continent whose youth was so august. Now, a line of fire runs through our country from East to West, and more than half a million men confront each other with hostile arms! Villages are burned; farms are deserted; neighbors are at bloody variance; industry stands still through fifteen States, or only forges implements of war; the sky at night is red with camp fires,—by day the ground trembles with the tramp of armies; yet amid many great and undeniable evils which every Christian patriot must bitterly lament, there are eminent reasons for thankfulness, several of which I shall point out to you.

I. Since we must accept this war with all its undeniable evils, it is a matter for thanksgiving that the citizens and lawful government of these United States, can appeal to the Judge of the Universe, and to all right minded men to bear witness, that this is not a war waged in the interest of any base passion; but truly and religiously in the defence of the highest interests ever committed to a nation's keeping. It is not on our side a war of passion, nor of avarice,—God is judge!—nor of anger; nor for revenge; nor of fear; nor of jealousy, as if to cripple a dangerous rival. We hold that the territory of these United States is common to all its inhabitants, and is not simply a possession, but a trust, and unless by deliberate decision of the people, lawfully assembled, and constitutionally expressed, it can never be abandoned, alienated, nor partitioned. We hold it in trust for the future!

Is it the duty of New York to defend its own territory against foes without or evil men within, from the Lakes to Montauk Point? Is it the duty of each New England State to defend every foot within its jurisdiction? In like manner and for the same reasons it is the duty of all the States collectively, to maintain the integrity of the national domain. It is not a question of whether we will or will not. Until by appointed and proper methods of the constitution it has been taken from our hands, it remains in them; not subject to our volition, but binding us by that silent oath that every man swears who comes to years of maturity and citizenship, to maintain inviolate the territory of these United States. It is the duty of the citizens also, to stand up for their government; to protect its righteous authority; to maintain all its attributes, and to see to it that its jurisdiction is not restricted, except by those methods which have been predetermined and agreed upon in that constitution on which it stands. But in our particular case the reasons for maintaining the government in all its ample jurisdiction are intensified beyond all measure, by the fact that the dangers which are threatened it, arise confessedly and undeniably not from the perversion of the principles of the constitution in our hands, or from oppressive administration of this government under those principles; but because a large body of men, gradually infected with new political doctrines, in their nature irreconcilable with the root principle of our government, have determined to overthrow it, that they may change its fundamental principles! We are not left to infer this. There is this merit in Southern politicians, that they are frank and open in the declaration of political doctrines. The best head among them is Mr. Stephens, and he declares in the most emphatic manner, that the object of the rebellion is to introduce new principles in the government instead of the old. I shall read:

"The new constitution puts at rest *forever* the agitated question relative to our peculiar institution."

(Mr. Beecher.—We shall see whether it is *forever.*) "African slavery as it exists among us—the proper status of the negro in our form of civilization. This was the immediate cause of the late rupture and present revolution. Jefferson, in his forecast, had anticipated this as the 'rock upon which the old Union would split.' He was right. What was conjecture with him, is now a realized fact. But whether he fully comprehended the great truth upon which that rock stood and stands, may be doubted. The prevailing ideas entertained by him and most of the leading statesmen at the time of the formation of the old constitution, were, that the enslavement of the African was in violation of the laws of nature, that it was wrong in principle, socially, morally and politically." (Mr. Beecher.—I thank him for that testimony.) "It was an evil they knew not well how to deal with, but the general opinion of the men of that day was that, somehow or other, in the order of Providence, the institution would be evanescent and pass away. The idea, though not incorporated in the constitution, was the prevailing idea at the time. The constitution, it is true, secured every essential guarantee to the institution while it should last, and hence no argument can be justly used against the constitutional rights thus secured, because of the common sentiment of the day. Those ideas, however, were fundamentally wrong. They rested upon the assumption of the equality of races. This was an error. It was a sandy foundation, and the idea of government built upon it; but when the 'storm came and the wind blew, it fell.' Our new government is founded upon exactly the opposite ideas." (Mr. Beecher.—I thank him for that acknowledgment.) "Its foundations are laid, its corner-stone rests upon the great truth, that the negro is *not* equal to the white man;"—(Mr. Beecher.—What an acknowledgment for a government)—"that slavery, subordination to the superior race, is his natural and normal condition. Thus, our new government is the first in the history of the world based upon this great physical, philosophical, and moral truth." (Mr. Beecher.—And I will take the liberty so far to interpolate his speech as to say, it will be the last. Farther on, Mr. Stephens says,—it is excellent reading, so that I cannot deny myself the pleasure of reading it to you)—"May we not, therefore, look with confidence upon the ultimate acknowledgment of the principle on which our government rests. It is the first government ever instituted upon principles in strict conformity to nature, and the ordination of Providence, in furnishing the materials of human society. Many governments have been founded on the principle of certain classes; but the classes thus enslaved, were of the same race, and in violation of the laws of nature. Our system contains no such violation of nature's laws. The negro, by nature and the curse of Canaan, is fitted for that condition which he occupies in our system. The architect, in the construction of buildings, lays the foundation with the proper materials—the granite, then comes the brick or the marble. The substratum of our society is made of the material fitted by nature for it, and by experience we know that it is the best, not only for the superior, but for the inferior race, that it should be so. It is, indeed, in conformity with the Creator. It is not for us to inquire into the wisdom of his ordinances, or to question them. For his own purposes he has made one race to differ from another, as he has made 'one star to differ from another in glory.' The great objects of humanity are best attained when conformed to his laws and decrees, in the formation of governments, as well as in all things else. Our confederacy is founded upon principles in strict conformity with these laws. 'This stone which was rejected by the first builders, is become the chief stone of the corner in our new edifice.' "

These last words, you will remember, were spoken by the Lord Jesus Christ, when set at naught and rejected by the Jews, his countrymen; and the Vice-President of these so-called Confederate States does not hesitate to declare, with infamous effrontery, that slavery, based on no other law than this, that slaves are of a different race: "that slavery stands in our system in the place in which Jesus Christ stands in the Christian scheme:" has become the head of the corner. Dr. Smyth, of Charleston, second to none in influence and learning among them, declares, " What is the difficulty and what is the remedy? Not in the election of Republican Presidents. No! Not in the non-execution of the fugitive slave bill. No! But it is back of all these. It is found in that atheistic red republican doctrine of the Declaration of Independence. Until that is trampled under foot there can be no peace." Allow me to say, until that is trampled under foot or its *antagonist*, there can be no peace. Which is to go under, time will show. I might multiply testimony. It is needless. The matter, so far from disguise, is the pride and boast of that boastful land. This, then, mark you, is a rebellion not against an oppressive administration, or against the principle of equal justice, of the fundamental right of liberty in every man who has not forfeited it by crime. That miserable subterfuge, that we hold, because all men are equal, that all men are therefore of one degree of power! It never has been pretended at all. We hold that men are as children are before a father; not equal in talent, nor wealth, nor opportunity of usefulness in the employment of their various endowments; but this: that every child, strong or weak, has a right to claim the same *kind* of justice, the same *kind* of chance that the other has; and we hold that all mankind, born black as night, or white as daylight, have the right to the free and unobstructed use of those powers of body and of mind that God Almighty endowed them with, and in this sense are equal—in their rights equal; and it is declared without equivocation or discussion, that the war is brought upon us—the revolution and war—because our government contains this false principle. It is a rebellion against this principle of government, and the people of this nation are aroused to *defend* their Constitution and their Government, not simply because it is assailed, but as if Providence meant to make this conflict illustrious in the annals of the world, because it is assailed in those very respects in which it embodies the latest fruit of Christianity, and the last attainment of modern civilization. The very things which belong to our own age in distinction from any which ever went before it—*these* are the very things which have been singled out and made the object of attack. We would defend our Constitution at any rate, but when it is charged with the noblest principles as with a crime, it appeals to every conscience and every heart in this land with a solemnity as of the day of judgment for its defence. In view of these facts, that are not hidden at home nor abroad, what are we to say of that amazing charge of Earl Russell, late Lord John Russell, where in an express manner he declares, that this is not a conflict, although originating in slavery, for it or against it? Although it involves, somewhat, commercial interests, yet he declares positively it is not a question of tariff. It is only, he says, one of those conflicts that have been waged so many times before in Europe—a conflict on the one side for empire and on the other side for power. He sees only an ambitious, selfish conflict, waged between two sections with respect to territory and dominion. We repel, with just indignation and with glowing pride, the amazing charge. We are contending not for that part of our Constitution which Justinian gave us, nor for that which came in any way from Rome, expressing justice as it was developed in that iron-hearted realm; but that which Christianity gave us, and which has been working out for eighteen hundred years. The principle in the conflict is the very one which gives unity to history. It is that golden thread which leads us through the dark mazes of nearly two thousand years, and connects us with the immortal Head of the Church. It is the principle of man's right based on the divinity of his origin. It is on that ground that all are brothers, and all alike stand on one great platform of justice and of love. That has been the struggle of eighteen hundred years, and this principle has been embodied in our Constitution, and this, with singular infatuation and clarity, the exponent of Southern views declares to be the very point of offence in our Constitution, and says, in unmistakable language, and with blasphemous illustration, that it is against that attribute that they are in arms to-day. Is there no cause for thanksgiving, then, that since we must war, God has called us to battle on ground so high, for ends so noble, in a cause so pure and for results so universal? For this is not a battle for us alone. It is so in our times: that every great deed, nobly done, is done for all mankind. The Potomac is the river of the earth, and battles there for our

Constitution, because it is a document of liberty, are the world's battles, and we are fighting not for our own liberty, but for those ideas which are the breastworks of liberty throughout the whole world, and there is not a man who bears the chain, there is not a man—serf, yeoman, slave, or what not—that has not an interest in the conflict, that we are set in God's providence to wage against these momentous doctrines of gigantic iniquity! There is honey in that lion.

II. It is a matter of thanksgiving that we have no sought this war, but by a magnanimous course have endured shame and political loss and disturbance the most serious, rather than to peril the Union. Indeed, I am bound to say, that so strong had the national feeling been with us, and so weak with them, that what they trod under their feet with contempt we have made an idol of, and like idolators, had thrown ourselves down at the expense of our very self-respect, at the feet of our idol of the Union. I do not mean that it would have been wrong to have taken the initiative in the cause which employs this conflict; but if, when the end is right and the cause sacred, it can also be shown that there has been patient and earnest and long-continued effort to seek the right by peaceful methods, by reasoning, by merciful appeal, and that the most desperate of remedies—war, has been forced upon us, not sought, not wished but accepted reluctantly, forced upon us by the overt act of rebellion, and is not either of our wish or procuring, *then* this patience and forbearance and reluctance to war will give an added lustre to our cause. I make these remarks out of respect to the Christian sentiment of nations. Contiguity is raising up a new element of power on the globe, and we do not hesitate to pay a just respect to the opinions of the Christian church and philantrophic people of other lands, and we stand boldly before earnest peace men, the kind advisers, the yearning mediators, yea, and before the body of Christ, his Church on earth, to declare; that this war, which we could not avert without giving up all that Christian civilization has set us to guard and to transmit, cannot on the other hand be abandoned without betraying every principle of justice, and of rectitude, and of liberty.

We do not fear search and trial before the tribunal of earth in the end. Those who should have given sympathy, but have given hatred, chilling advice, and ignorant rebuke, shall yet confess their mistake, and our fealty to God and to Government and to mankind.

When it would have swelled our sails, there was no breath of applause or sympathy. When the gale is no longer needed, and our victorious voyage is ended, we shall have incense and gales of admiration enough.

But meanwhile, God has called us to war upon a plan so high as never feet, I think, trod before; and though we did not want it, and prayed against it, and with long endurance sought to avert it and avoid it, now it has come it is an infinite satisfaction to know that we can stand acquitted before the Christianity of the globe in such a conflict as this. There is honey in that lion.

III. It is a matter of thanksgiving that this even promises to solve those difficult problems which have baffled the wisdom of our wisest counsellors. There stands in the Vatican at Rome a marble prophecy of America. A noble and heroic man; on either side a lovely son; but all, father and sons, grasped in the coils of a many time's enfolding serpent, whose tightening hold not their utmost strength can resist and with agonized face Laocoon looks up, as if his anguish said, "Only the gods can save me, whose hate I have offended."

So sat America. Around this Government and around the clustered States, twined the gigantic serpent of slavery; but here let the emblem stop. Let us hope another history awaits us than that of the fabled Greek. There have been secret and open reasons—many, that have made slavery a most unmanageable thing in our national counsel.

Had it been desired to test to the uttermost the power of republican institutions to sustain good government, no other conceivable trial can be imagined that would do it as this has and will. It gathered up in its coils almost every one of those unmanageable elements, each one of which is accounted a match for human wisdom in other times.

An inferior race, a foreign race, separated from us by physiological signs and badges of the most marked character; a people whose nation brought in the element of climate, and whose existence, in the relations of government, fed every one of the fiercer passions, and touched but few of the moral sentiments, and these but feebly; educating men to idleness, avarice, lust and pride of dominion. Thus these poor African bondmen, in all their helplessness and weakness, were cast into this nation's troubles, with difficulties of caste, of race, of condition, of climate, difficulties which the strongest and wisest knew not how to endure! War seems likely to clear up the question which politics could not touch. By our organic law, we were forbidden to meddle with local institutions, and though they were infecting the national veins with their poison, though we saw that from these local institutions general and national influences were going forth, yet our organic instrument would not permit us to lay our hand upon them.

We could not bring to bear the moral forces by which other evils are met. There was no public sentiment that could wrestle with slavery; partly because no public sentiment can ever avail against the blinding passions. There is not in all the broad globe a moral influence that is of direct omnipotence—there is not an influence on the broad globe that can resist; that can for a moment stand the charge of the aroused passions of the masses of mankind. The bottom of the head is ten thousand times stronger than the top of the head, in the race and in the world. There was also sectional pride and jealousy which prevented our access to the South by any public sentiment. There was more than that. There was that inevitable ignorance which must come where the few are owners, and the mass are poor and dependent. There were both also political and commercial influences which were dividing us—insidiously dividing good men one from another, and making it impossible to raise any public sentiment, except a tempestuous one, which could do no good. And so we were drifting—the North more clear for liberty every year—the South more determined for slavery, and by that very fact each having less and less influence with the other.

Now it has pleased God by the very infatuation of these people rudely to dash these two sections together. But this conflict can procure emancipation in no such way as England is pleased to propose, as the condition of her sympathy,—by direct politically conferred emancipation. England speaks and says,—not her lion, that I think in these latter days has a touch of doubt,—England speaks and says, "If you will make this a war for a principle, I will be with you. If you will make this a war for emancipation, then we will give not only sympathy and prayer, but all needed succour."

It was not by England's sympathy that we became independent; it was not by her advice that we became her equal, and we shall perhaps be able to settle our troubles without England's sympathy. For one, I am not so ungenerous as to lay up anything, and I am not so ungenerous as to remark against the race and stock from which I am proud to have come; but when we have such sublime leadings of God's providence, and England, with the voice of her curmudgeon, assumes to proffer sympathy or advice, I do not hesitate to say to her,—Remain at home! We will do our own work, and you shall be spectators.

But one thing, however, we will have from her. I say it in the face of England before her time, and she cannot help herself—there is one thing we *shall* have from her yet. In the coming end, when all our troubles are settled, we shall have their admiration and then their sympathy, and then, after a while, we shall live on, just as we have before, only a good deal better; but meanwhile, however much it may hurt us, or alarm us, or grieve us, we are bound to say that we are going to trust in God, and get along without England.

Of all the advice which has been given, while it may seem to those who know not the facts or nature of our institutions, the most direct and rational, and yet of all advice given, there is none which chimes more with Northern popular impulse than this, to make a declaration of emancipation to settle this difficulty. But neither popular feelings, nor foreign advice can be followed. We must conduct this war, my friends, *by and through our institutions*, or else we must declare that our institutions have failed and we have reverted to original principles—one or the other of these courses.

The last we cannot and shall not do. We are not going to say to the world that Republican institutions have so signally failed, that we have abandoned them, and are going for the war to go back and re-establish other ones. No man will say that. If, then, we are fighting for our Constitution, we must not violate it ourselves. A pretty thing, to make war against them for violating the Constitution, when we are willing to violate it ourselves! We may not congressionally declare emancipation. I wish we could! I wish we could! I wish Adam had not sinned, and his posterity had not been affected; but that does not help the matter, as I can see. I wish our fathers had stood out against what are called the compromises of the Constitution. Better then than now. The serpent just hatched is not half as much to be feared as the full grown serpent, and our troubles have grown with every generation. But what is the use of sighing? That isn't it. We cannot reject the Constitution. We have lived under it—have declared our fealty to it. Can we now break the compact, though we seek even so magnificent a result as the emancipation of the slave?

Shall we rend the crystal instrument—the joy of the world and our pride? It is a very easy thing to say, "It is a state of war, let us declare emancipation." It is n't on our part a revolution. We stand in our institutions. We believe in them. We administer the war by them; in consonance with their spirit and their forms; and we must. We cannot, by destroying the Constitution, accomplish these desirable ends. If any ask me whether a law or constitution is superior to original principles of morality or justice, I say no. But plighted faith is in the nature of a moral principle. It is one of the original principles. Our faith is given; we must keep it. When we cannot abide by our promise, then in methods expressly provided, we must withdraw the pledge and agreement, and withdraw constitutionally and stand apart as two separate peoples.

Are we, then, shut up by these reasonings? No, we are not. What the pen of legislation cannot do, the sword of war will do. What we could never have liberty to do, they themselves have afforded us the means of doing, and thrust upon themselves; and there never was an instance in which condign punishment has followed the step of trangression more surely than is seen in this, that having made war for the maintenance of slavery, they have brought down on their heads its destruction.

Let us see. The Southern strength in this self-imposed war, is slavery. They have placed their system as a bulwark, and are fighting our Constitution behind that. And now, so it has come to pass, by their own selecting and arrangement, that we are not able to fulfill our sworn compact and duty, and maintain the integrity of this land and Constitution itself, according to its own forms and in consonance with our oath, except by defending them against those who assail them with the shield of slavery on their arms, and in open transgression. We shall strike through their shield. It is not a political act, but a military necessity which they have brought upon themselves, and beginning emancipation we will carry it to such a degree, as to make slavery a burden to them, and, at least, we will make them most earnest in the end to put an end to it. But look now at the effect of emancipation in war—not in violation of the Constitution, but according to it; for if men rebel against government, by that crime they forfeit life itself and much more, property and standing; and by revolution they have forfeited their lives and property according to local law, and that property according to the declaration Scripture has made, if not wings, yet feet, and run away—much of it.

The government must take these fugitives in some way into its hands. What do we behold! Either one of two things; that men that have been set free by no act of their masters, and by no superior authority, men now, not in scores but in hundreds and thousands, are held by our government; only six months ago slaves under local law, men, women, and children, now, by a law self-imposed, they have gone out from under local laws. The government now holds them. How? As men, or captives? Where can you find law or constitutional forms that will permit these fugitives to be treated as other than men? Where is there any article that will give the right to the Government to look upon these as any other than men? You may call them contrabands, you may invent with dexterity whatever term you choose. The Southern law that called them slaves is broken, and they have now come into possession of the Government of the United States, to be nothing else than men. They are emancipated, and there are to-day thousands upon thousands of emancipated men in the possession of the Government, which is bound to treat them, if not as citizens yet as men!

Be pleased to consider what disturbance the system must have; and as our armies progress, step by step, what swarms will rise up, just as soon as liberty is given them. It is a little puzzling to me, having heard it said by so many good men, that this patriarchal institution begets such a love between master and slave that they would not take liberty as a gift, to observe the infatuation which seems to have seized, in the disorderly affairs of our nation, these blessed creatures, so that they prefer the bondage of liberty, to the liberty of bondage. It seems so strange I can hardly account for it unless it be on the supposition that there was some mistake in the premises. I suspect that the African does after all love liberty; though I do not doubt that curled hair, black skin, and curved spines make great political differences, yet, I suspect in one thing the African is still like the Anglo-Saxon. They are both of God, and the touch which God left on them and in them is there; not on their face, but invisible; and every creature formed after God's image, how base soever he may be, longs to be free.

In so vast a system, so loosely compacted, and so subject to fevers and inflammations, the very disturbance of it, the disturbance of the occupations of the slaves, turning them away from their regular fields, and the reasons why they are so turned away, which must needs break into their darkened minds, inuring them to work for purposes of manhood, all these are educating them to be free. They are preparing the way. But that is not all. The South has consented to pay a premium of about $200,000,000 on free cotton. There was never such stupendous liberality since the world began. The South has said to the world —"If you would like to outbid us in the market, we have been making our wealth out of cotton, rice, &c., but nevertheless we will agree to tie our hands up for two years; we will not appear in the markets of the world. Take that premium and raise these products," and meanwhile India and China are raising them, and all the world to-day is raising them. There seems to me a picture of beauty in that justice by which cotton on this shore invited cotton from Africa. Cotton from Africa shall yet strike off the shackles from the bondmen in America, and as cotton made slavery cotton shall cure it.

When then, the government progressing by its arms from State to State, shall have accepted slaves of those States that have been in arms,—and this is the true doctrine and the only one which I can understand,—one which is constitutionally permissible, one which is forced upon us by the act of rebellion, and by the necessities of war, viz., confiscating the property of men in arms against the government, and that will be the property of by far the largest number of slave owners, and the government will soon own more slaves than those that are left. Now, the first duty the government can have, will be to have a provisional government adapted to these emancipated slaves. This government is not going, I take it, to put them up at auction.

Our government has got to do something with them. There is going to be a United States government for freemen in the South. There is going to be a national government over the nation's freemen right by the side of the national government over slave men. There are going to be two antagonistic governments together. How will they work? See what they have done. They have compelled us in defending the Constitution to extend its Ægis over their slaves. They have compelled us to bring down, right into their midst, a new form of provisional government for wants which they themselves have created. Do you suppose the slave system is going to stand on such a firm foundation as it has in days past? I fancy that its days are ended, and just as fast as we are able to take care of them, God will put them into our hands.

Before the African is permitted to swing back the mysterious portal and step into life, God, by means of his own, has provided means of meeting his wants and taking care of his infancy, just as the mother is God's provision for the wants of an infant child. Now God never prepares a future birth of a multitude, any more than of an individual, without having prepared a bosom on which it may lie, and food which it can eat, and provision has been made for this race as it is coming into its new condition. Where there is a want there is a supply already provided. Let me then express again, as a matter of the most profound thanksgiving, that although the steps and appliances by which emancipation is to be completed are not apparent, we see the direction in which it is travelling, and from which we believe it will come!

What we could not do politically, they have given us the liberty of doing by the arm of the military. What is more: when this great struggle is past, it will lay the foundation of a peace firmer than we have had before.

1. Because it must extinguish that pestilent heresy of the sovereignty of individual States. We are not thirty crowned sovereigns sitting in voluntary council together; we are thirty united States, whose general union and local independence are both alike immutable. The government cannot take away the local authority, and States cannot take away the general authority of the government, and one is as immutable as the other. Our political troubles came through this heresy. Slavery is the cause, but State independence was the crevice in which the powder was sifted which would have exploded this goverenment, and it must, therefore, be made burglar-proof, by stopping up those cracks, and when they touch off their powder again, it will be all outside.

2. It will bring into better acquaintance and respect the North and the South. They have hitherto met chiefly in only two places, and that very little of late. The South have come to Saratoga and Newport and other watering places, and I must beg leave to say, that what they see when they come here is not what we should be willing to present as specimens of the North. Our summer rabble at the great watering places are not a fair index of New England families, nor of the Northern community. The other place where they meet is in the halls of Congress, and heaven forbid that it should be thought that those men represent us!

But now we have sent a representative which we are quite willing should march through the South to tell them what Northern men are, and what Northern men mean to do. Since they as a mass cannot read, we must give them vocal instruction.

Since they would not come to our school, we must send our schoolmasters to them, and revive again here, on a larger sphere, the old peripatetic system, by which philosophers walked, and their disciples went with them. By the time our armies have gone through the Southern States, I think there will be a thorough change of public sentiment of the South in respect to the manhood, courage and power and resources of the North, and I tell you without sarcasm and without *double entendre*, it is on this that I expect there will yet stand a peace in times to come, that we never had and never could have had before. They have not respected or they have not understood your civilization; for such is the inevitable condition into which slavery brings the white man, that they cannot understand the elements belonging to Northern civilization.

The thing which will at last inoculate them is the *mailed fist*, and that which you cannot tell them by word of mouth you can by a smite of the hand. There are some things that parents do not tell their children, except in the act of discipline. Moral ideas sometimes come through the skin, and there never was an instance in which the community needed more to be instructed in the language in which they were born and they themselves speak, than the Southern community, and when they find that you are courageous and more than a match for them in arms, from that moment they will respect you, and when there is a better understanding of each other there will be a better chance for peace, and although just at present there is neither understanding nor respect, nor any particular evidence of peace, yet I think that the corn is growing that shall yet wave with those kernels in its ear.

IV. There are likewise causes of rejoicing on account of the Providential benefits which have surrounded and accompanied this struggle thus far.

1. If this war had broken out before, I know not how we should have been able to maintain it.

I shudder when I look back at the condition of the North! If ten years ago this struggle had been forced upon us, our foes would have been those of our own household. But what a change! What a vast improvement has been made in the Northern States by the enlightening of the Northern conscience, and in the uniting of the people since 1850, and not until we were in some sense prepared did God permit the accomplishment of these events which have brought to pass this crisis, and how it is a matter of profound thanksgiving that we are a united North. I do not mean that there are no reptiles that lurk in their holes and hiss, but I do mean that they no sooner put their heads above the earth than they are scotched.

I doubt not there are many men who would do mischief if they could, but the North stands like the old Apostle, who, while throwing fuel on the fire, a viper fastened on his hand, and when the spectators looked that he should die, saying, "he is a criminal escaped from justice," behold he shook it off and suffered no harm, and they thought he was a God afterward.

First they thought he was a culprit, and then a deity, and so the North, standing by this fire and warming itself and casting on fuel, finds on its hands some vipers; yet it shakes them off and suffers no harm. We are a community infrangible, indivisible, and, as sure as the sun rises and sets, victorious!

2. Nor are we to forget that, as the stars in their courses fought against Sisera, so there have been great natural agencies in this great conflict, that have been co-oporating with us. Who that shuddered at the crisis of '57, knew that God was saying to us:—"Take in your sails, put your ship in order, a hurricane is about to fall on you." Nevertheless, we put the ship in good condition, and now that the storm has come we understand the reason of the warning. There never was a time when the North could so well afford as now, to have a storm upon us; for, although individual men are falling down, the community was never so rich; never in condition to bear the burden of war so well as now.

3. Nor is that all: When war had come, it pleased God to say to the winds and the rain, that travel far and near, fulfilling his purpose, "Make the earth teem with plenty, breed grain in the clod. He that made

the seven years of plenty and the seven years of famine, made two years of superabundance and plenty with us, to take the crown from the head of cotton and put it on the head of grain.

For what? Because this had been their peculiar boast, "Cotton is King, and by this power we will bring France with her haughty Emperor, and England to our terms, and we will crush the North by the fleecy sceptre of cotton."

We did not know it. God knew it. I walked through all the cornfields, and heard the leaves rustling, and, ignorant soul that I was, I thought it was the wind sweeping through the corn, and did not understand the messages, but it was God speaking to me in the rustling corn, which now I understand, though before I knew it not, and every field throughout the North lifted up its long sword blades, prefiguring the victorious swords, and every one that came through said, "Liberty is coming, emancipation is coming. Corn shall dethrone cotton, for now just when mechanical England would have demanded our ports to be opened—what? She needs our grain more than she needs Southern cotton. She must feed her men before she gives their hands anything to do, and we come nearer starving them than the South comes nearer clothing them. So the Emperor too has just been obliged to send into his minister the declaration that he has laid aside his material prerogative to open fresh budgets of expense, that he will restrict himself, and that the nation may economise.

In other words, just at the time when we are enjoying boundless prosperity, France is obliged to curtail her army, and to save in every possible matter. We have good guarantees for peace there, and we have good guarantees for peace in England. This thing is going to be fought out by ourselves. We have sealed five thousand miles of coast; we have shut their breathing holes, and now we are putting the red hot torch of war at the other end, and in a short time victory will be determined, and while we are carrying on this war, God is loading up magazines for us. God has poured money into our coffers. But let all nations stand off! Sweep around the ring and stand off spectators, and now let these gigantic forms stand,—Liberty and God—Slavery and the Devil, and no more put hand or foot into that ring until they have done battle unto the death! Amen. Even so, Lord God Almighty, it is Thy decree; this Thy purpose; and when victory shall come; "not unto us; not unto us," but in the voices of thrice ten thousand ransomed ones mingled with all Thy children, "unto Thy name shall be the praise and the glory, forever and ever, amen."

www.ingramcontent.com/pod-product-compliance
Lightning Source LLC
LaVergne TN
LVHW020742120826
845150LV00010B/2343